The Mirror of Life

The Journey of Self-Discovery

FRANK ASAMOAH, BBA, MBA

Dedication

To all seekers of truth and purpose,
May the reflections in the Mirror of Life Guide you on your journey
of self-discovery and illuminate the path to your true essence.

***

To my beloved wife, Mrs. Akpene Asamoah, and our precious daughter, Trinity (Nana Yaa) Asamoah, affectionately known as Baby Trini,

Your unwavering love, support, and understanding have been my guiding light throughout this journey of writing and sharing. You both inspire me to reach for the stars and pursue my dreams with passion and dedication. May God bless and establish us for a brighter day and night, filling our lives with boundless joy, love, and prosperity.

***

This dedication is also extended to every young person out there, every reader who picks up this book, seeking inspiration, guidance, and wisdom on their own path to success. May God bless you abundantly and grant you the desires of your heart.

Acknowledgment

I extend my deepest gratitude to those who have supported me throughout the creation of this book. To my family, whose unwavering love and encouragement have been my guiding light, I am eternally grateful. To my friends and mentors, thank you for your invaluable insights and inspiration. To the readers who embark on this journey with an open heart and mind, I dedicate these words to you.

Contents

Introduction

In this breadth of life, each of us is but a speck of light amidst the darkness. Yet within the depths of our being lies a universe waiting to be explored—a universe mirrored in the reflections of our own lives.

If you are listening or reading "The Mirror of Life-" by Frank Asamoah, it is not by accident but by divine orchestration to provide you with the information needed to help you develop an intentional lifestyle that will propel you to live a life of purpose, harmony and abundance .

Permit me to journey with you to reflect and discover your true purpose by the renewing of your mind to understand the timeless wisdom of the mirror of life. In the following pages, we will embark on a quest to uncover the hidden truths of our existence, confront our fears and doubts, and embrace the fullness of our potential.

At the heart of this exploration lies the concept of Ikigai— the Japanese principle of finding purpose and meaning in life. As we delve into the depths of our own reflections, we will discover the harmony between what we love, what we are good at, what the world needs, and what we can be rewarded for.

Through practical steps, actionable strategies, and profound insights, we will learn to harness the power of self-reflection and introspection. We will confront our inner geniuses head-on, embracing them as allies on the path to self-awareness and growth. And we will emerge from this journey with a renewed sense of hope, purpose, and have the readiness to embrace the fullness of our life with clarity and conviction.

So, let us gaze into the Mirror of Life together and let its reflections guide us towards our true essence. For within its depths lies the key to unlocking the secrets of our souls and embracing the beauty of our existence. Enjoy the journey.

Abstract

The Mirror of Life: is a profound exploration of life's stages and the transformative power of self-reflection. Through the metaphor of a mirror, I will guide you on a journey of self-discovery, encouraging you to confront your fears, acknowledge your strengths, and embrace your true purpose. This book is divided into chapters corresponding to different age brackets, each offering practical insights, actionable steps, and thought-provoking reflections to help you navigate life in stages with clarity and purpose.

Key Frequently Asked Questions (FAQ's) and Answers:

1) What is the central concept of "The Mirror of Life by Frank Asamoah ?"

The central concept revolves around using the metaphorical mirror to reflect on your innermost thoughts, desires, and aspirations. It is to encourage you to view your life as a journey of self-discovery, where introspection and self-awareness are essential tools for growth and fulfillment.

2) How does the book address different age brackets?

The book is structured into chapters corresponding to various age ranges, from childhood to old age. Each chapter delves into the unique challenges, opportunities, and lessons associated with that particular stage of life, offering practical advice and actionable steps tailored to the needs of readers in that age bracket.

3) What are some practical exercises provided in the book?

The book includes exercises such as gazing into a literal or metaphorical mirror to reflect on one's thoughts, emotions, and desires. It also encourages readers to envision their ideal selves and set specific goals to align their actions with their aspirations. Additionally, there are exercises focused on self-assessment, goal-settings to embracing journey of self-discovery.

4) How does "The Mirror of Life" emphasize the importance of self-awareness?

The book emphasizes that self-awareness is the cornerstone of personal growth and fulfillment. By encouraging readers to confront their fears, doubts, and insecurities it empowers them to gain insight into their true identity and purpose. Through self-reflection and introspection, readers can unlock their hidden reserves of strength, creativity, and potential.

5) What role does the metaphor of the mirror play in the book?

The metaphor of the mirror serves as a symbol of self-discovery and reflection. It prompts you to peer beyond the surface and delve into the depths of your life. By viewing your reflections not as mere images but as the mirror of your innermost selves.

1

The Mirror of Life Concept

In the beginning was the word, the word was with God, and the word became flesh to live among men. These profound words serve as a reminder of the power of creation and the journey of life. Success, as we perceive it, is not merely an endpoint but rather the peak of processes and experiences that shape our character and define our path.

Why is it that some individuals undergo a significant transformation upon achieving wealth or success? Often, it is because they lose the sense of urgency and hunger that once drove them forward. They forget the lessons learned in the pursuit of their dreams and become complacent in their newfound comfort.

This chapter is dedicated to a new beginning in your life, for anyone who stands on the threshold of their journey, poised to make their mark in this world. It is a call to action, urging you to embrace the challenges and opportunities that lie ahead with courage and determination.

Greatness, as we understand it, is not solely measured by external achievements but rather by the quality of one's thinking. Your mind is limitless, capable of transcending any obstacle or limitation placed before you. Remember, you have the power to become anything you desire—the divine spark within you is alive and waiting to be ignited.

As we reflect on the journey of life, it becomes evident that every milestone, whether it be a birthday, a new job, a wedding, or even a divorce, is but a fleeting moment in the grand wall of existence. What truly matters is the process—the experiences, the lessons learned, and the growth achieved along the way.

It is imperative that we teach the reality of our mortality and instil in the younger generation a sense of responsibility and resilience. Life is a precious gift, and while none expected to die young, we must acknowledge the fragility of our existence and cherish each moment with gratitude and joy.

To the young and hopeful, I say this: embrace each day with a smile, for it is through optimism and perseverance that you can overcome any challenge that comes your way. Let us strive to build, mold, and mentor one another, fostering a community of love, respect, and unity.

Remember, you are not alone on this journey. Your parents, whether chosen by fate or divine orchestration, are there to guide and support you. Treasure the gift of their presence and honor their sacrifices as you strive for greatness.

As we embark on this journey together, let us commit to bringing forth a generation that is more powerful, intelligent, and compassionate. For in nurturing the potential of our young ones, we sow the seeds of a brighter future for all mankind.

At the core of this exploration lies the profound concept of Ikigai—the Japanese principle of discovering purpose and meaning in life. Ikigai teaches us to seek harmony among our passions, skills, societal needs, and rewards. On this journey, the mirror becomes a symbol of self-discovery, inviting us to delve beyond the surface and into the depths of our being.

The Mirror of Life encourages you to perceive your reflections not merely as images but as mirrors of your inner selves. It urges us to confront our fears, doubts, and insecurities directly, recognizing them as stepping stones on the path to self-awareness and growth in raising the next generationals leaders. Through the mirror's lens, we gain insight into our true identity and purpose, illuminating the way forward with clarity and conviction for the young.

Life, reflects the energy and intentions we project onto it. It mirrors our thoughts, beliefs, and actions, serving as a gauge of our inner state. When we approach life with positivity, gratitude, and authenticity, we create a ripple effect that resonates with those around us. By embracing the mirror of life, we become catalysts for change, inspiring the best in ourselves and others through our words and deeds.

Self-mastery lies at the heart of this journey, empowering us to seize control of our destinies and shape our realities of the young. Through the power of self-reflection and introspection, we gain the wisdom and insight necessary to navigate life's challenges with grace and resilience. We can unlock our latent reservoirs of strength, creativity, and potential through practical steps and actionable strategies.

Action Exercise:

Gaze into the Mirror: Take a moment to peer into the mirror, both literally and metaphorically. What do you observe reflected back at you? Notice the thoughts, emotions, and desires that surface.

Envision Your Ideal Self: Visualize the person you aspire to become —the embodiment of your deepest values, passions, and aspirations. What steps can you take today to align your actions with this vision? Set specific goals and intentions to propel you toward your highest potential.

Embrace Self-Discovery: Commit to embracing the mirror of life as a tool for self-discovery and growth. Embrace each positive or challenging reflection as an opportunity for learning and evolution. Remember, the journey towards self-awareness and fulfillment begins with a single step— take that step today, and let the mirror of life guide you towards your true purpose.

Through these actions, may you embark on a transformative journey of self-realization and fulfillment guided by the timeless wisdom of the Mirror of Life as you grow with your young one.

Notes

2

Be Transformed (0-10 Years)

The journey through life's mirror begins in the tender years of 0 to 10, a phase where the foundation of your character is laid. This period is pivotal, as the reflections seen and interpreted by young minds shape their understanding of themselves and the world. The Mirror of Life, at this stage, teaches you the fundamental values of love, kindness, empathy, and curiosity. It is a time for planting seeds that will grow into the robust trees of their future selves.

For Parents and Guardians: Understanding Your Role

Parents and guardians play an indispensable role in molding these young reflections. It is crucial to recognize that every interaction, every word, and every emotion displayed acts as a stroke on the canvas of a child's personality. This formative period is less about direct teachings and more about creating an environment that encourages positive self-reflection.

Love and Security: The primary reflection a child should see is one of unconditional love and security. A secure attachment forms the basis for healthy emotional and psychological development, teaching children to trust themselves and their caregivers.

Positive Role Modeling:

Children imitate what they see. Exhibiting behaviors that reflect integrity, respect for others, and self-discipline serves as a live demonstration of what those values look like in action.

Encouraging Curiosity:

A curious child is a learner for life. Encouraging questions, exploration, and discovery fosters a love for learning. The world is a vast place, and through a child's eyes, every aspect of it is a part of the Mirror of Life, reflecting back lessons and wonders.

Embracing Mistakes:

It is essential to teach children that mistakes are not failures but opportunities for growth. Reflecting this attitude toward errors helps children develop resilience and a positive attitude toward challenges.

Action Plan for Parents:

Create a Loving and Secure Environment: Regularly express love and affection. Ensure your home is a safe haven where your child feels secure, both physically and emotionally.

Be the Mirror You Wish Them to Reflect:

Demonstrate the values you wish to instill. Let your actions and words mirror the qualities of kindness, empathy, patience, and resilience.

Foster Open Communication:

Encourage your child to express their thoughts and feelings. Listen actively and validate their emotions, helping them build self-esteem and communication skills.

Cultivate Curiosity:

Provide diverse experiences—books, nature walks, museum visits, and artistic activities. Each new experience is a piece of the mirror, reflecting back lessons and sparking curiosity.

Set Boundaries with Love:

Effective discipline involves setting clear boundaries and consequences out of love, not anger. It teaches children self-discipline and the concept of natural consequences.

Celebrate Individuality:

Recognize and celebrate your child's unique talents and interests. Supportive encouragement helps children develop a strong sense of self and confidence in their abilities.

Practice Gratitude and Mindfulness:

Introduce simple practices of gratitude and mindfulness, teaching them to appreciate life's blessings and live in the moment. These practices enrich the reflections in the Mirror of Life with positivity and peace.

In nurturing these young souls, remember that the goal is not to create a reflection that is perfect but one that is whole, balanced, and true to itself. The Mirror of Life, in these formative years, should teach children to view themselves with kindness, curiosity, and resilience, laying a solid foundation for the transformative years to come.

Notes

3

The Curiosity (10 - 20 Years)

The decade spanning from 10 to 20 years of age is marked by an insatiable curiosity, a quest for understanding that propels the young mind into a world of endless possibilities. It is a period characterized by rapid growth, not just physically but intellectually and emotionally. The Mirror of Life, during these formative years, reflects a spectrum of potential selves, inviting exploration and discovery.

The Essence of Curiosity

Curiosity is not just a desire to know; it is a call to adventure, a challenge to push beyond the boundaries of current understanding. For those navigating this crucial decade, it is vital to recognize that curiosity is a double-edged sword. It can lead to great discoveries and insights but can also veer toward distractions and pitfalls if not guided wisely.

Understanding Limitations and Possibilities

At this age understand that your actions have consequences, and while exploration is encouraged, you must navigate your curiosity with responsibility. You will be held accountable by your actions and inactions, your involvement in harmful behaviors, yielding to peer pressure, or neglecting your education—should be clearly distinguished from the things you can do, such as pursuing new hobbies, developing skills, and fostering healthy relationships.

Making a Difference Through Purposeful Thinking

To truly make a difference, it is essential to think purposefully. This means setting goals that are not only ambitious but also meaningful. Young people should be encouraged to ask themselves: "How can my actions today shape a better tomorrow?" This reflective questioning is crucial for developing a sense of purpose and direction.

Practical Steps for Purposeful Growth

Set Clear Goals: Encourage setting specific, achievable goals. How much is enough. Remember, everything is related. The law of relativity states that every person will experience challenges as an opportunity for growth, to strengthen our characters.

The difference between those with goals, and those without. Those with goals knows where they are going. So long as you are intentional and deliberate. You will surely attract what the goodness of life brings.

Understand that nothing is too big, nothing is too small. A billion dollar is not enough, likewise one dollar. I want you to dream big, and in so doing be intentional and deliberate to be successful. This should be challenging yet realistic, fostering a sense of accomplishment and direction.

Embrace Learning: Adopt a growth mindset, understanding that intelligence and talent are just starting points. Learning from failures and setbacks is part of the journey.

Practice Delayed Gratification: Teach the value of waiting for a more rewarding outcome rather than seeking immediate pleasure. This skill is crucial for long-term success and satisfaction.

Seek Mentorship: Encourage relationships with mentors who can offer guidance, wisdom, and support. These relationships can provide valuable insights and open doors to new opportunities.

Engage in Reflective Practice: Regularly reflect on actions, decisions, and outcomes. This practice fosters self-awareness and helps align actions with personal values and goals.

"To succeed, jump as quickly at opportunities as you do at conclusions."

– Benjamin Franklin.

This quote encapsulates the essence of curiosity—being swift to explore opportunities but cautious in drawing conclusions without sufficient reflection and understanding.

Scripturally, Proverbs 4:7 reinforces the value of wisdom and understanding: "Wisdom is the principal thing; therefore get wisdom: and with all thy getting get understanding."

Curiosity, guided by wisdom and understanding, can transform the mirror of life into a canvas of endless possibilities. For the young and the old, this chapter serves as a reminder that curiosity, when navigated with purpose and caution, becomes the compass that leads one to a life of fulfillment and meaningful impact.

Notes

23

4

The Morning of Life (20 -30 Years)

"The early bird catches the worm, but it's the second mouse that gets the cheese."

- Anonymous

This contradictory quote captures the essence of the morning of your life, a period between 20-30 years, with a nuanced reminder: while early efforts are crucial, strategic patience and learning from the initial trials of others can also lead to success. This stage, related to the early hours before the workday begins, is saturated with potential and promise, demanding seriousness, discipline, and a proactive stance to navigate the complexities of personal and professional growth.

Ten Guiding Principles for Navigating the Morning of Life: Insights for Ages 20 -30.

1. This period between 20 to 30 indeed is the morning of life, it's full of opportunities to seize your carol moment and potential to explore. It is a time when many lay down the foundation for their future, be it personal, spiritual and professional.

2. Embrace the dawn of your journey, for within the early hours of life lie boundless opportunities awaiting your grasp. Navigate the complexities of growth with resilience and curiosity, for it is in this morning light that you shape the contours of your future.

3. As the sun rises on the canvas of your existence, let the age of 20 to 30 be the palette with which you paint the masterpiece of your life. Each brushstroke represents a decision, each color a choice; wield them wisely, for the morning is ripe with potential.

4. In the garden of your youth, tend to the seeds of ambition and curiosity with care. For it is during the age of 20 to 30 that these saplings take root, blossoming into the trees that will bear the fruits of your endeavors in the seasons to come.

5. As the morning mist lifts, so too does the veil of possibility unfurl before you. Seize the dawn of your adulthood with courage and conviction, for within these early hours lie the seeds of greatness waiting to be sown.

6. Like a symphony at daybreak, let the age of 20 to 30 be the overture to the grand opus of your life. With each note

played and each melody woven, compose the harmonies of your personal and professional growth, knowing that the dawn holds infinite promise.

7. Amidst the cacophony of choices and challenges, remember that the age of 20 to 30 is your canvas, your stage, your blank sheet of music. Embrace the rhythm of life's symphony, conducting each movement with intention and purpose, for it is in these early hours that the melody of your destiny is crafted.

8. As the curtain rises on the stage of adulthood, let the age of 20 to 30 be your debut performance. With courage as your spotlight and ambition as your script, take center stage and dance to the rhythm of your aspirations, for the world is your audience and the morning light, your stage.

9. Embrace the dawn of your twenties with the fervor of a sunrise, for within these early hours lies the opportunity to sculpt your identity and forge your path. Let each decision be a brushstroke on the canvas of your existence, painting a portrait of resilience, growth, and purpose.

10. the crucible of youth, where dreams are tempered and ambitions take flight, let the age of 20 to 30 be your forge. Mold your aspirations with the fires of passion, shaping them into the instruments of your success, for it is in this furnace of growth that greatness is born.

Actionable Exercise:

Mapping Your Morning

Reflect and Journal: Spend a week journaling your daily activities, noting which actions contribute to your long-term goals and which do not. Identify patterns or distractions that can be minimized.

Set a Vision Board: Create a vision board that represents your goals for this decade. Use images, quotes, and symbols that resonate with your ambitions and place it where you'll see it daily.

Skill Audit and Development Plan: Conduct a self-audit to identify the skills you need to acquire or improve. Develop a plan to learn these skills, whether through online courses, workshops, or by finding a mentor.

Practical Steps to Harness the Morning

Cultivating Seriousness and Discipline:

Routine is Your Ally: Establish a morning routine that aligns with your goals. Whether it's reading, exercising, or planning your day, make sure it contributes to your personal and professional development.

Embrace the 5-Second Rule: Hesitation can be a significant barrier to action. Practice the 5-second rule by Mel Robbins; when you have an impulse to act on a goal, count down 5-4-3-2-1 and physically move or do something to achieve it.

Adopting a Proactive Approach:

Networking: Actively seek networking opportunities within and outside your field. Attend conferences, join professional associations, and participate in online forums to connect with potential mentors and collaborators.

Preemptive Learning: Anticipate the skills and knowledge needed in your field's future landscape. Start learning them today to stay ahead of the curve.

Seizing Opportunities:

Stay Alert: Opportunities are often disguised as more work, challenges, or failures. Stay open and alert to these disguises by adopting a growth mindset that views every experience as a stepping stone.

Volunteer Strategically: Offer your skills to projects or roles that align with your career path, even if they are outside your current job description. This exposes you to new learning opportunities and people who can potentially open doors for you.

Setting and Achieving Goals:

SMART Goals: Ensure your goals are Specific, Measurable, Achievable, Relevant, and Time-bound. This framework guides you in setting realistic targets and measuring your progress.

Accountability Partners: Share your goals with a trusted friend or colleague who can help keep you accountable. Regular check-ins can increase your motivation and help you stay on track.

Inference:

The morning of your life is a fleeting yet transformative period. It is a time to build, to learn from the early attempts (be it yours or others), and to strategically position yourself for the opportunities that lie ahead. Remember, the morning sun may rise slowly, but its light gradually illuminates everything in its path. By adopting a blend of seriousness, discipline, and a proactive mindset, you can ensure that when the sun fully rises on your life, it shines on a foundation built to last and thrive.

Actionable Next Step: Start tomorrow by implementing one of the actionable exercises. Let this act as the first step toward maximizing the morning of your life, ensuring that by the time the sun comes up, you are well on your way to achieving your dreams.

Notes

32

5

The Afternoon of life (30 -40 Years)

"The true harvest of my life is intangible - a little star dust caught,
a portion of the rainbow I have clutched."

- Henry David Thoreau

As the sun dips lower, casting long shadows and bathing the world in a golden glow, so too does one enter the reflective period of life's evening, the years between 30-40. This chapter unfolds the essence of reaping the harvests sown in the morning of your life and the significance of each grain of effort, discipline, and aspiration.

Reflect on Past Achievements

Actionable Exercise: Dedicate a moment for reflection each day. Keep a journal of achievements, both small and large, to visualize the progress you've made. This act of recording and reflection fosters gratitude and a deeper understanding of your journey's value.

Practical Steps:

Catalogue Achievements: List down your achievements since your 20s. Recognize and celebrate each milestone, understanding the journey's worth beyond mere outcomes.

Assess Learned Skills: Reflect on the skills and knowledge you've acquired. How have these shaped your personal and professional growth?

Embrace Growth: Identify areas of personal growth and how challenges have sculpted your resilience and character.

Taking Stock of Harvest and Investments

Actionable Exercise: Conduct an annual review of your life's 'portfolio.' Evaluate your career trajectory, relationships, health, and personal development. This holistic review will highlight areas of abundance and those requiring nourishment.

Practical Steps:

Financial Review: Assess your financial investments, savings, and expenditures. Are they aligning with your long-term security and goals?

Career Evaluation: Reflect on your career path. Are you progressing towards your aspirations? What steps can you take to align your career with your passions and goals?

Relationship Audit: Examine the health and value of your relationships. Cultivate those that bring joy and growth, and reassess those that do not.

Personal Development: Look into your personal growth investments, such as education, hobbies, and health. Ensure they are contributing positively to your well-being.

Celebrating the Fruits of Your Labor

Actionable Exercise: Create a celebration ritual or tradition that honors your achievements. It could be a simple dinner, a quiet evening of reflection, or a gathering with loved ones.

Practical Steps:

Acknowledgment: Take time to acknowledge your hard work and perseverance. Recognizing your efforts is crucial for emotional and mental well-being.

Gratitude Practice: Cultivate a practice of gratitude. Regularly express thanks for your achievements, the people who've supported you, and the opportunities that have come your way.

Share Your Journey: Inspire others by sharing your experiences, struggles, and successes. Mentorship is a powerful way to give back and celebrate your journey.

Planning for the Future

Actionable Exercise: Set aside a day for strategic life planning. Visualize where you want to be in the next decade, identify the steps needed to get there, and break these into actionable goals.

Practical Steps:

Goal Setting: Define new personal and professional goals. Use your past achievements and current aspirations to chart a path forward.

Skill Development: Identify new skills or knowledge areas to pursue that align with your future goals. Lifelong learning is key to continuous growth and adaptation.

Balance and Wellness: Plan for balance. Prioritize activities and goals that support your mental, physical, and emotional health.

Inference

The evening of life between 30-40 years, is not an endpoint but a vibrant chapter of reflection, celebration, and forward-looking planning. It's a testament to the mornings spent in pursuit of dreams and the noons navigating the sun's zenith. With the wisdom gleaned from past seasons, you're poised to embrace the twilight with grace, purpose, and anticipation for what's yet to unfold.

Notes

6

The Night Is Drawing Nigh (40 -50 Years)

"Evening is a time for reflection, a chance to account for the day's journey and prepare for the following night. It's in this preparation that we find our true worth."

- Unknown.

As the twilight of our careers and the early stages of elderhood approach, those in the age bracket of 40-50 years find themselves on the precipice of significant life transitions. This chapter, "The Night Is Drawing Nigh," serves as a guide for navigating these shifts with grace, intentionality, and foresight. Here, we delve into the essential tasks of taking stock of life, making necessary adjustments, preparing for a graceful exit, and embracing wisdom and fulfillment. This chapter is not for the weak.

Taking Stock of Life

Begin by conducting a comprehensive review of your life's journey thus far. Reflect on your achievements, your unfulfilled aspirations, the quality of your relationships, and your overall sense of well-being. This reflection should be honest and objective, aimed at understanding the alignment between your life's actions and your deepest values.

Actionable Steps:

Reflective Journaling: Dedicate time each day to journal about your experiences, noting achievements, regrets, and lessons learned.

Feedback Gathering: Seek feedback from trusted friends, family, and colleagues about your impact and legacy thus far.

Life Audit: Create a life audit chart that includes various aspects of your life, such as career, relationships, health, and personal growth. Rate your satisfaction in each area and identify where adjustments are needed. Learn to celebrate the little wins.

Making Necessary Adjustments

Upon taking stock, it's crucial to pivot where necessary. This may involve career changes, revitalizing or ending certain relationships, adopting healthier lifestyle habits, or realigning your daily actions with your core values. If you want change, you must go for it.

Actionable Steps:

Goal Reset: Based on your life audit, set new, realistic goals that reflect your current priorities and dreams. It must be ten times inspired by you. No one else is going to do it for you. You hold the keys to make it happen!

Skill Development: Identify and begin learning new skills that align with your adjusted goals and interests. Culture is dynamic, and change is difficult. Learning new skills may seem late, but it's better late than never. Consistency is key, so developing a strategy to make it happen should be your goal. Finish what you start.

Health Overhaul: Implement a comprehensive plan for physical and mental health, including diet, exercise, and mindfulness practices.

Preparing for a Graceful Exit

Looking ahead, preparation for retirement and the eventual end of life should be approached with meticulous care. This involves financial planning, estate planning, and considering the legacy you wish to leave behind.

Actionable Steps:

Financial Planning: Meet with a financial advisor to discuss retirement planning, savings, investments, and estate planning. Maybe, you have already done this in the early stage of your life. Revisit, check the portfolio and keep making it happen.

Legacy Planning: Reflect on the values and impact you want to leave behind. Begin writing your memoirs or documenting your life lessons for future generations.

Legal Affairs: Ensure that all legal documents, such as wills, trusts, and advance directives, are in order and up to date. You never know what tomorrow brings. You are a soldier and must be ready to defend and uphold your legacy for the next generations.

Embracing Wisdom and Fulfillment

This stage of life is ripe for embracing the wisdom gained through years of experience and finding fulfillment in mentoring others, engaging in meaningful activities, and appreciating life's simpler pleasures.

Actionable Steps:

Mentorship: Offer your expertise and guidance to younger individuals within your professional or personal community. Life is a marathon, and the ability to pass on the experience is a great essential for posterity.

Volunteerism: Engage in volunteer work that aligns with your values and passions.

Mindfulness and Appreciation: Cultivate a practice of mindfulness and gratitude, focusing on the present moment and appreciating the journey of life.

Inference

"The Night Is Drawing Nigh" is not merely a chapter of closure but one of transformation and legacy-building. By taking stock of life, making necessary adjustments, preparing for the future, and embracing wisdom, you can navigate this pivotal stage with purpose, leaving a lasting impact on the world and setting the stage for a fulfilling and graceful exit.

Notes

7

The Shadows of the Evening (50-60 Years)

"As the shadows lengthen, we are reminded not of the light that has passed but of the luminance that lies within."

- Unknown

The ages between 50 and 60 serve as a prelude to the twilight years; a period often likened to shadows that grow longer as the sun sets. This chapter, titled "The Shadows," delves into this critical decade of life, focusing on the importance of resource assessment, future investments, preparation for unforeseen circumstances, maintaining a positive mindset, and embracing new opportunities. Through practical strategies, this guide aims to illuminate the path for you to navigate the complex transition into retirement and beyond.

Assessing Your Resources

The foundation of navigating the shadows effectively lies in a thorough assessment of your resources. This encompasses a critical review of your financial health, physical and mental well-being, social connections, and personal fulfillment.

Actionable Steps:

Financial Review: Conduct an annual review of your retirement savings, investments, and any debts. Consult with a financial advisor to optimize your financial plan for retirement.

Health Check-up: Prioritize regular health screenings and adopt a healthy lifestyle that includes balanced nutrition, regular exercise, and mental health care.

Social Network Analysis: Evaluate your relationships and commit to strengthening bonds with family and friends. Expand your social network by joining clubs or groups aligned with your interests.

Personal Fulfillment Audit: Reflect on your passions and hobbies. Consider how you can integrate more of what fulfills you into your daily life.

Investing in Your Future

Investing in your future is critical during this decade, ensuring you have a solid foundation upon which to build your retirement years.

Actionable Steps:

Retirement Planning: Maximize contributions to your retirement accounts and explore other investment opportunities to diversify your portfolio.

Skill Development: Engage in lifelong learning by taking courses or pursuing hobbies that challenge your mind and body.

Estate Planning: Regularly update your will and estate plan, ensuring that your legacy is preserved according to your wishes.

Preparing for the Unknown

The future is inherently uncertain. Preparing for the unknown is a prudent strategy to mitigate unforeseen challenges.

Actionable Steps:

Emergency Fund: Ensure you have an adequate emergency fund to cover unexpected expenses.

Insurance Review: Regularly review your insurance policies (health, life, long-term care) to ensure they meet your current and future needs.

Flexibility in Plans: Develop a flexible mindset toward retirement planning, recognizing that adaptations may be necessary as circumstances change.

Maintaining a Positive Mindset

A positive mindset can significantly impact your ability to navigate this decade with resilience and grace.

Actionable Steps:

Gratitude Practice: Cultivate gratitude by maintaining a daily journal of things you are thankful for.

Mindfulness and Meditation: Engage in mindfulness practices or meditation to reduce stress and enhance your emotional well-being.

Positive Social Interactions: Surround yourself with positive influences and seek out communities that uplift your spirits.

Embracing New Opportunities

The shadows of life can also cast light on new opportunities, offering a chance to explore uncharted territories of personal growth and fulfillment.

Actionable Steps:

New Ventures: Consider turning a long-standing hobby into a small business or volunteering in roles that utilize your expertise.

Travel and Exploration: Use this time to travel, explore new cultures, and gain new perspectives.

Mentorship: Offer your knowledge and experience as a mentor to younger individuals in your profession or community.

Inference

The period between 50 and 60, "The Shadows," is a time rich with potential for growth, reflection, and preparation for the future. By assessing your resources, investing in your future, preparing for the unknown, maintaining a positive mindset, and embracing new opportunities, you can navigate these years with purpose and joy.

This chapter sets the stage for entering retirement not just with readiness but with a sense of excitement for what lies ahead, ensuring that the shadows cast by the setting sun are met with the light of wisdom, experience, and anticipation for the next chapter.

The Shadows" evoke a unique phase in life, where the sun sets on one's career and casts a different light on the path ahead. It's a juncture where time seems both abundant and fleeting, prompting introspection on one's accomplishments, dreams, and aspirations. Amidst the uncertainties of aging, there's an opportunity to redefine success and fulfillment, transcending societal expectations and embracing personal truths.

As we stand at the threshold of this transformative period, it's essential to recognize the power of resilience and adaptation. Life's journey unfolds in unexpected ways, presenting challenges and opportunities that shape our character and perspective. By embracing change with openness and courage, we harness the potential within us to navigate the shadows with grace and resilience.

Moreover, "The Shadows" symbolize a transition from ambition to meaning—a shift from chasing external validation to cultivating inner wisdom and authenticity. It's a time to prioritize relationships, experiences, and passions that bring profound joy and fulfillment. Through introspection and self-discovery, we uncover the true essence of our being and forge deeper connections with ourselves and others.

Furthermore, "The Shadows" beckon us to cultivate a spirit of gratitude and appreciation for the richness of life. Every experience, whether joyful or challenging, contributes to the mosaic of our existence, imbuing it with depth and resonance. As we embrace the wisdom gleaned from our journey thus far, we illuminate the path forward with a renewed sense of purpose and gratitude.

In essence, "The Shadows" represent not an end but a new beginning—an invitation to embrace the beauty of life's twilight and welcome the dawn of a new chapter with anticipation and hope. By honoring the lessons of the past, embracing the present moment, and envisioning the possibilities of the future, we illuminate our path with the radiance of wisdom, resilience, and boundless potential.

Notes

8

The Strength, Weakness, and Perfection (60-70 Years)

"In their advanced years, they shall still bear fruit; they shall stay fresh and green,"

(Psalm 92:14)

A verse that beautifully encapsulates the essence of life between 60-70 years. This age bracket is marked by a profound season of reflection, gratitude, and the cultivation of a legacy that resonates with the wisdom of a life lived fully. In this chapter, we delve into the intricacies of strength, weakness, and the pursuit of perfection, aligning with the natural progression of life's journey as it comes full circle.

Strengths in the Golden Years

The golden years are rich with the strength of accumulated wisdom and experience. It is a time when the fruits of one's labor can be enjoyed and shared, embodying the biblical principle that "A gray head is a crown of glory; it is found in the way of righteousness" (Proverbs 16:31). The sharing of wisdom, mentoring the younger generation, and volunteering contribute not only to societal well-being but also to personal fulfillment, reinforcing one's sense of purpose and legacy.

Self-care and personal growth emerge as paramount during these years. The focus shifts towards nurturing one's physical, mental, and emotional well-being, embracing the importance of self-reflection as echoed in Lamentations 3:40, "Let us test and examine our ways, and return to the Lord!" This period allows for introspection and the embracing of life's full spectrum, cherishing each moment and the growth it brings.

Weaknesses and Regrets

Yet, with reflection may come regrets or acknowledgments of weaknesses—missed opportunities or paths not taken. Ecclesiastes 7:3 posits, "Sorrow is better than laughter, for by the sadness of face the heart is made glad." This suggests that confronting our sorrows or regrets can lead to deeper joy and appreciation for life's blessings, teaching us to live more fully in the present and forgive ourselves and others for past transgressions.

Perfection and Legacy

The pursuit of perfection has been redefined in these years. It becomes evident that life's value is not measured by flawlessness but by the love shared, the wisdom imparted, and the kindness spread. It's a time to embody the principle that "He has made everything beautiful in its time" (Ecclesiastes 3:11), acknowledging that each phase of life, with its unique imperfections, contributes to the beauty of our existence.

Building a legacy becomes about the meaningful impact made on the lives of others, the strength of one's character, and the virtues upheld. It's less about material wealth and more about the richness of one's contributions to the fabric of humanity, encapsulated in the exhortation to "lay up for yourselves treasures in heaven" (Matthew 6:20).

What to Do and Not to Do

In navigating this pivotal decade, certain practices can enhance well-being and fulfillment:

Do maintain a healthy lifestyle: Prioritize physical activity, balanced nutrition, and restorative sleep, adhering to 1 Corinthians 6:19-20's call to honor one's body as a temple.

Do cultivate meaningful relationships: Invest in relationships that enrich the soul, understanding that "Two are better than one" (Ecclesiastes 4:9) for they can uplift and support one another through life's journey.

Do reflect on your life: Engage in introspection, appreciating the journey thus far and contemplating how best to utilize the gift of your remaining years, embodying Psalm 90:12's wisdom, "So teach us to number our days that we may get a heart of wisdom."

Do embrace new experiences: Seek out new horizons that foster growth, embodying the spirit of exploration and continuous learning.

Conversely:

Do not dwell on regrets: Recognize and learn from past mistakes but remain anchored in the present and hopeful for the future, following Philippians 3:13 -14's guidance to forget what lies behind and strain toward what lies ahead.

Do not neglect self-care: Remember the importance of caring for your spiritual, mental, and physical well-being, ensuring that you are well-equipped to enjoy and fulfill God's purpose for your life.

In this stage of life, as we come to terms with our strengths and weaknesses and as we strive not for perfection but for a meaningful existence, we are reminded that life, in its essence, is a precious gift. Let us then approach each day with a heart of wisdom, seeking to leave a legacy that glorifies God and enriches the world around us.

Likewise, amidst the complexities of life's journey, it's crucial to embrace a mindset of forgiveness and grace. Holding onto grudges or harboring resentment only weighs us down, hindering our ability to fully embrace the present moment. By extending forgiveness to ourselves and others, we liberate ourselves from the chains of bitterness and open our hearts to experience the fullness of love and joy.

Furthermore, in this stage of life, we are called to cultivate a spirit of generosity and service towards others. As we reflect on our blessings and privileges, we recognize our responsibility to uplift and empower those around us who may be less fortunate. By sharing our time, resources, and talents with compassion and kindness, we sow seeds of hope and transformation in the lives of others, leaving a lasting impact that transcends our own existence.

Moreover, as we journey through "The Shadows," we are reminded of the impermanence of life and the importance of cherishing every moment to share our light to enlighten others. Time is a precious commodity, and how we choose to invest it defines the legacy we leave behind. Let us, therefore, approach each day with intentionality and mindfulness, savoring the simple joys and embracing the beauty of life's fleeting moments.

Additionally, as we navigate the complexities of aging, it's essential to cultivate a spirit of curiosity and lifelong learning. Embrace new experiences, embark on adventures, and challenge yourself to step outside your comfort zone. By embracing a growth mindset and remaining open to new possibilities, we continue to evolve and thrive, enriching our lives with depth, meaning, and purpose.

"The Shadows" beckon us to embrace the fullness of life, weaving together moments of joy, sorrow, growth, and transformation. As we navigate the ebb and flow of life's journey, let us do so with courage, grace, and a steadfast commitment to living a life of purpose and significance.

Overcomers' motivational and life transforming books that have enrich my life and trust it will be of great benefit to you as well!

The Happiness Advantage, Shawn Achor

As a Man Thinketh, James Allen

Multiple Streams of Income, Robert G. Allen

Debt Free for Life, David Bach

Smart Women Finish Rich, David Bach

The Automatic Millionaire, David Bach

Rich Dad Poor Dad, Robert T. Kiyosaki and Sharon L. Lechter

Cashflow Quadrant: Rich Dad's Guide to Financial Freedom, Robert T.

Kiyosaki and Sharon L. Lechter

Think and Grow Rich, Napoleon Hill

Acres of Diamonds, Russell H. Conwell

Outliers, Malcolm Gladwell

The 7 Habits of Highly Effective People, Stephen R. Covey The

Richest Man in Babylon, George S. Clason

How to Win Friends and Influence People, Dale Carnegie Success

for Teens, by the Editors of the SUCCESS Foundation

SUCCESS.com

All You Can Is All You Can Do, But All You Can Do Is Enough, Art Williams

Breaking the Rules, Kurt Wright

The Science of Getting Rich, Wallace D. Wattles

Conversations with Millionaires, Mike Litman, Jason Oman, et al

The 21 Irrefutable Laws of Leadership, John C. Maxwell Cultivating and Unshakable Character, Jim Rohn Failing Forward, John C. Maxwell

The Power of Positive Thinking, Norman Vincent Peale You Can If You Think You Can, Dr. Norman Vincent Peale You Were Born Rich, Bob Proctor Pathway of Success, Mensa Otabil

Victory! Brian Tracy

Jewish Wisdom for Business Success, Rabbi Levi Brackman/ Sam Jaffe My Vision, Muammar Gaddafi

My Vision, Mohammed bin Rashid Al Maktoum

Falsesafe-Leadership, Matthew Ashimolowo

Master, Robert Greene

The Art of Seduction, Robert Greene

Starting Your Own Business, David Lester

How they started in tough times, David Lester and Beth Bishop How they started Global Brands, Edited by David

Notes

10

The Crown of Serenity – Ages Between 80-100 Years

"The glory of young men is their strength, gray hair the splendor of the old."

- Proverbs 20:29

As the final chapter in the grand tale of life unfolds, those aged between 80 and 100 years find themselves adorned with the crown of serenity. This period, often heralded as the twilight of twilight, is a time of profound reflection, deep familial bonds, and a serene acceptance of life's ultimate journey. In this chapter, we delve into the beauty of growing old surrounded by grandchildren, the comfort of unwavering family support, the simplicity of clean garments, and the peaceful anticipation of a graceful exit.

Basking in the Glory of Grandchildren

The presence of grandchildren brings a unique radiance to the golden years. Their laughter, innocence, and boundless energy infuse life with a renewed sense of joy and purpose. Through their eyes, the elderly witness the wonders of the world afresh, reliving cherished memories and imparting timeless wisdom. As Psalm 127:3 declares, "Children are a heritage from the Lord, offspring a reward from him," underscoring the divine blessing grandchildren represent in the twilight of life.

Embracing the Warmth of Family Support

In this chapter, the family becomes the cornerstone of solace and support. Through the ebbs and flows of life's journey, the bonds forged with loved ones deepen, offering a sanctuary of love, care, and understanding. Family members become pillars of strength, providing comfort, companionship, and assistance in navigating life's challenges. Ecclesiastes 4:9-10 encapsulates this sentiment: "Two are better than one... for if either of them falls down, one can help the other up."

Savoring the Simplicity of Clean Garments

The act of donning clean garments takes on a symbolic significance in the twilight years. It reflects a commitment to dignity, self-respect, and the acknowledgment of life's inherent beauty. Each clean garment serves as a testament to a life well-lived, adorned with moments of joy, sorrow, and everything in between. As Isaiah 61:10 proclaims, "I delight greatly in the Lord; my soul rejoices in my God. For he has clothed me with garments of salvation and arrayed me in a robe of his righteousness."

Awaiting a Peaceful Exit

In the final pages of life's narrative, the elderly awaits a peaceful exit with a sense of tranquility and acceptance. They embrace the inevitability of mortality with grace, recognizing it as the culmination of a life richly lived. Surrounded by loved ones, they find solace in the knowledge that their legacy will endure through the memories, values, and traditions they imparted. As Psalm 23:4 assures, "Even though I walk through the darkest valley, I will fear no evil, for you are with me; your rod and your staff, they comfort me."

Conclusion: The Crown of Serenity

The journey between 80 and 100 years, the "Crown of Serenity," is a testament to a life imbued with grace, wisdom, and love. It is a time to bask in the joy of grandchildren, embrace the warmth of family support, savor the simplicity of clean garments, and await a peaceful exit with tranquil acceptance. This chapter represents the culmination of a life well-lived, adorned with the splendor of gray hair and the radiance of a heart filled with love. In the twilight of twilight, the crown of serenity shines brightly, illuminating the path to a legacy that transcends the boundaries of time itself.

NOTES

About The Author

As an author and friend, his fervent hope is to guide you toward the shores of success and fulfillment. He want you to embark on this odyssey of self-discovery with courage, conviction, and unwavering determination. For in the mirror of our youth lies the blueprint for a future adorned with the laurels of excellence and the crown of self-actualization

He is highly motivated entrepreneur, visionary leader, and a motivational speaker dedicated to empowering individuals to achieve their highest potential. As a first-generation graduate, completed his primary education at New Edubiase Methodist Primary School, Assiamah Oguahyia Junior High, and New Edubiase Senior High. He then earned his Bachelor's degree in Business Administration from the esteemed Methodist University Ghana and his MBA in International Business from the prestigious Brandeis International Business School in the United States.

Frank's impressive educational background, combined with his extensive experience in entrepreneurship and leadership, makes him a highly sought-after speaker and mentor in the business and academic communities. His commitment to excellence and innovation has earned him numerous accolades and recognition for his outstanding contributions to the field.

Through his engaging and dynamic presentations, Frank inspires and motivates individuals to pursue their passions and achieve their goals. His unique perspective and insights into the world of business and entrepreneurship offer valuable lessons and guidance for aspiring professionals seeking to make a difference in their respective fields.

He is an exemplary role model and leader who embodies the values of hard work, dedication, and perseverance. His achievements serve as a testament to the power of education and the limitless potential of the human spirit.

Frank spent most of his life in Ministry as a youth leadership advocate growing up. He is the founder and CEO of Generational Youth Development Network, which is based in Ghana, and the founder of Meet Professionals LLC, based in the USA. Frank has a passion for personal development and a commitment to lifelong learning. He shares his insights and experiences to help others navigate through life's journey uniquely.

Frank currently resides in Massachusetts, U.S. When he's not writing or speaking, Frank enjoys spending time with his family, traveling, and exploring new adventures.

Join Frank Asamoah on a journey of inspiration, motivation, and transformation. Let this be your guide to unlock your full potential.